MW01603036

American Art Quilts
Quilt 21

2   0   0   2

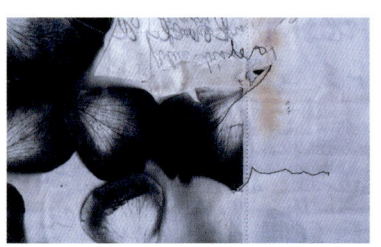

American Art Quilts

Quilt 21

2 0 0 2

A national juried exhibition

QUILT 21 PRESS
LOWELL, MASSACHUSETTS
2002

Quilt 21 Director: Maxine Farkas

Library of Congress Card Number: 00-191184

First Edition
©2002, Quilt 21 Press

ISBN 0-9701915-1-0

Quilt 21 Press
The Brush
256 Market Street
Lowell, MA 01852, USA

All photography by the artists unless noted below:
David Caras 28, 58, 70, 80, 84; Sam Brewster 48;
Pol Leemans 44, 72; Tech Photo & Imaging 32, 40;
Avec Langridge 30; Cliff Fenton 78; Seth Tice-Lewis
56; Joe Ofria 64; Keith E. Martens 22; Neal E.
Collett 50; Maddog Studio 82; Ken Sanville 24

Design by Higgins & Ross
Printed by Mercentile/Image Press
Cover Art by Joan Schulze

DEDICATION

To Michael Decker, Gay Tracy, Bill Giavis,
Cynthia Hughes, Carol Boileau,
dear friends whose unfailing support
makes this exhibition possible.
And to the memory of Berna Finley
who believed when few others did.

ACKNOWLEDGMENTS

This exhibition and catalogue are supported in part by the Lowell Cultural Council, a local agency, which is supported in part by the Massachusetts Cultural Council, a state agency.

We wish to thank E. Linda Poras, Executive Director of the Brush Art Gallery for allowing Quilt 21 to continue to be shown in the gallery.

Judith Lavine Smith and a Collector who wishes to remain anonymous remain our staunchest supporters.

Our thanks to Joan Schulze for allowing a detail of her piece 'The Cloisters' to be used for the cover of this catalogue.

And our deepest thanks to Quilt 21 co-founder Sandra Sider who, although it was necessary to give up formal participation in the management of Quilt 21, continues to provide valued encouragement and advice.

Corporate support has been provided by Bernina of America, Husqvarna Viking, and Pfaff.

Husqvarna VIKING

PFAFF

CONTENTS

PREFACE
Defining "Art Quilt"

Collectors and critics alike have come to value the fluidity and expressive qualities particular to fine art quilts, in which the sum of textile, color, and texture is much more than their individual components. Quilts take the images and color of prints and paintings into another dimension that is not quite sculptural, enticing the eye along lines of stitching drawn in and against the surface itself, often with three-dimensional embellishment. Art quilts take time to make and time to appreciate, with fine examples showing the viewer something new each time the light shifts. This experience does not necessarily happen in an exhibition of paintings and it often is absent from exhibitions of prints. It is why people travel significant distances to view art quilt exhibitions such as Quilt 21, for the delightful magic of these visual discoveries.

We are learning that many quilt artists have some sort of background in the arts, and that numerous quilt artists have studied with a small group of quiltmakers who have themselves had formal training in studio art. While folk art designs and traditional quiltmaking skills certainly have contributed to the growth of quilt art in the United States, a significant number of today's artists working in the medium of quilted surfaces have, in fact, earned their bona fide in art classes or by studying books about color, design, and technique. For political, practical, and aesthetic reasons, these individuals work primarily in textiles and fiber. They are artists first and quiltmakers second.

We may continue to disagree on what precisely an art quilt should be, but we now have an excellent idea of when a quilt is art. Defining "art quilt" is as pointless today as defining "painting." If the piece is primarily fabric and/or paper, includes stitching as a design element, and has the substance of more than a single layer of material, let's call it a quilt. In addition, the work can also be called a painting, or fiber sculpture, or even a mixed-media print. If it excites our eyes and provokes or satisfies our minds, then let it be called art.

Sandra Sider
Institute of Fine Arts,
New York University

INTRODUCTION

There is much that is new in this, the second, Quilt 21 catalogue; a new format, new sponsors, and most importantly, exciting new work.

The quality of submissions this year was uniformly high and, as a result, the jury process was extremely difficult. For 4½ days the 320 pieces that were submitted were viewed, discussed, reviewed, and discussed until a consensus was reached. And even then, all of the submissions were reviewed one last time to ensure that nothing had been overlooked. At the end of the process the jurors selected 35 works. Sixteen of the artists chosen had been exhibitors in Quilt 21/2000. A number of the new exhibitors have never before shown their work nationally. All of the work selected was deemed by the jurors to transcend material and process in the expression of the artist's vision.

We are delighted to have had the opportunity to expand the number of awards. At this writing we are making four awards, Jurors' Choice, Husqvarna Viking Award for 2002, Pfaff Artists' Award for Excellence (given to a piece chosen by the Resident Artists of the Brush Art Gallery where Quilt 21 is based). and the Bernina Award for Innovation in Machine Embroidery.

The new format designed by Joan Ross is the result of a grant from the Lowell Cultural Council.

The jurors for Quilt 21/2002 were Laura Cater-Woods, M.F.A., professional artist, curator, and teacher, and Maxine Farkas, M.A., professional artist, curator, and director of Quilt 21.

Maxine Farkas
Number 12
14" x 14"

Risk Taking, Art Making
Maxine Farkas

Fear manifests in many shapes and sizes, fear of falling, fear of the unknown, fear of flying. But of those fears which are learned early, the fear of failure is one of the greatest blocks to creativity. The statement 'I'm just not creative' is directly rooted in the belief that everything that one produces must conform to an externally defined scale of perfection. The fear of failure confines us to established paths. When the fear of failure is lost, much becomes possible. Exploration leads to experimentation. Experimentation can produce new and exciting work or dismal failure, the outcome is never certain until the work is done, the whole examined and assessed.

The willingness to take risks, explore new ground, to follow instinct and eye, to abandon that which is incompatible, to embrace critical review, to lay ego aside in deference to the work, is perhaps one of the primary attributes of successful engagement in the making of art.

Yet where there is risk, there is also reward. Experimentation in art can be a wondrous experience, it allows the artist to work without inhibition, to follow where curiosity leads. Often in the making of art there is much freedom, be it the freedom to explore personal demons or the freedom to play.

Joan Schulze writes of 'The Cloisters', "It is composed by taking an earlier work, cutting it up and recycling it to make a new quilt. This takes the idea of collage and extends it to a risky enterprise." To many, the idea of taking a sharp edge to finished work is anathema. For Schulze this process is a next step in the act of creation. In 'No Longer Safe', Loewenberg took a work of personal significance and with a sharp edge transformed it, to search for a response to September 11th.

Exploration of new ground can take many forms, for some it is the incorporation of a variety of print processes. Gillman in 'Urban Landscape' used a plethora of traditional and not-so-traditional printmaking techniques. Donabed utilized computer manipulated imagery in 'Coleus Mandela'. Colsh also manipulated imagery in 'Fall Line' and in 'Embers' with very different results.

For others the demarcation of new ground is accomplished by incorporation of new visualizations as in Jones' movement from the improvisational block which dominated his previous work to landscape in 'Night Falling.' San Chirico in 'Altar Fragments VI: Eclipse' advances the work by stripping of imagery to basic shapes and forms. For Nash in 'Particolare 6 and Particolare 7' it is the choice of portions of previous works to magnify. Upshaw in 'Worms and Holes I' moves

toward creating a less humorous, more serious body of work. Levin ommunicate experiences in 'Bilbao I.' Fenton explores an aesthetic negative space in 'Fences 9'.

There is much that is new in this exhibition, new directions for established artists and new expressions from many whose work is just beginning to become known.

Laura Cater-Woods
Echo #5 Fragment
24" x 27"

Conversation
Laura Cater-Woods

Kurt Vonnegut wrote "Art is one half of a conversation." He uses art as a noun. The object exists in time and space and independently of its maker. Vonnegut went on to say that if the artist wanted to know if what had made was, in fact, art, the artist should place it on a wall and then watch to see if anyone stopped to look at it. Vonnegut's criteria, then, was the capability of the object to engage the viewer. I suggest that art, as an object, is only one-third of a conversation. There is the dialogue of creative process between the maker and the object, and the dialogue between the object and the viewer. The art is the "medium," the language, between viewer and artist. With work that has the ability to engage the viewer for a prolonged time, conversations develop and change with each encounter. Rarely do we have the opportunity to discuss the work with the maker, but particularly successful art works lead us to believe that we have insight into the mind or experience of the artist.

The current Quilt 21 exhibition takes these conversations another step. Each piece was selected because it transcended its materials and process. The materials and the techniques,

rather than being the sum total of the piece, are part of the language used, the "voice" of the image. The voice varies from artist to artist. With each encounter we are drawn deeper into the imagery, coming to new understandings each time we see the work. Additionally, each of the works in the show speaks to the whole. The exhibit is a multi-leveled discussion, enriched by each speaker in turn.

The questions of medium and category have been part of the debate on art quilts during the last decade. In the effort to gain mainstream acceptance, artists working with this form have presented their work as mixed media, as collage, as cloth paintings and, often, as quilts. Critics have asked at times why a particular work was not in fact, a painting. Others have asked, was the work in fact a quilt? Artists have asked why these questions were necessary. Considering some core differences between painting and art quilts may help to clarify the question, and partially explain the power of the medium of cloth. Our ideas about stitched surfaces and cloth, conscious or not, become part of the conversation of viewing the art. We associate with "quilt" things that may not pertain to the image before us. When a given piece withstands or overcomes the gestalt of the viewer's associations, we move into a new area where the category is irrelevant.

Most paintings and drawings can be seen as tangible manifestations of vison in a moment in time and space, but works in cloth speak to experience over a span of time. Paintings and drawings, regardless of size or scale, can be made in a matter of hours, and their size is usually predetermined. Works in cloth, regardless of the spontaneity or improvisational method of the approach used, develop in an additive/subtractive process, slowly. Unlike paintings or drawings which can show the ephemeral nature of light, or the emotional gesture, compositions based in fabric must deal with light captured and absorbed, and gesture sustained and stilled. The passage of time in the making and viewing, combined with the inherent narrative quality of cloth, make even the most cerebral works an intimate experience (Autenrieth, Schulze) .

The voice of the cloth itself welcomes the viewer in a way that paint often does not.

This can be a great advantage, but can also become a trap for the artist unwilling to take risks. Staying within the confines of traditional geometric approaches to cloth constructions, or attempting to replicate painting or printmaking in the medium of cloth, are approaches which have the potential to confine the artist and stifle expression. Many of the artists in this exhibit use cloth as one part of the creative dialogue, but they also go beyond the surface. Manipulating fabric through various applied surface design techniques, (Dueul, Donabed, Gillman), deconstructing and recombining earlier pieces (Loewenburg, Schulze), using actual negative space (Fenton) and combining traditional drawing techniques with painterly fabric areas (Linet) are some of the ways these artists transcend the categories. Victoria Montgomery's graphite on cloth, "Cloth Sketches I: Passé," for example, layers planes with stitched and drawn line to give us a view of time and aging. By comparison, Denise Linet's evocative contour drawing, "Abstraction #4", presents the figure in a loose architectural space. The introspective arrangement of space asks us questions: what is seen, who sees, what is the relationship between the two?

Works seen in context of one another set up a different level of conversation. For example, the modernist, painterly approach of Dominie Nash's abstractions, juxtaposed with Dan Olfe's hard-edge composition or Phil Jones's lush surface can become a reflection on contemporary art history, seen through the lens of fabric. While each refers to colorist concerns, the way in which fibers are handled to build the pieces takes the formal issues into a more interesting dimension. The handling of the edges in Nash's pieces for example, contributes areas of transparency and blending while also speaking to the physical nature of the cloth and addressing the subject matter of the image.

The mark of the artist and his/her attitude is present in each piece. Process and materials effectively support content. Some works speak outwardly to the world (Trager, Jones, Gillman, Levin, Woock). Others (Forster, San Chirico, Linet) are more introspective. In "Fences 9" Claire Fenton uses the physical structure of the composition to create a metaphor addressing the borders we create and experience. When turned on the side the fences become ladders, offering an escape from the boundaries. The use of actual negative space speaks to the nature of the layered surface while adding an unexpected element. The fact of fabric, layers, and stitching as central to all the images in this exhibit, is secondary to the how the processes combine to express the unique vision of each artist.

Jurors' Choice Award
Joanie Gagnon San Chirico

My love of archeology and history has manifested itself in my Artifacts series, mystical pieces from a time long past, filled with legend and symbolism that are, at the same time, both ancient and modern. I'm sure that the relics of long ago can aid us in our struggle to make sense of our world for the future.

I have an insatiable curiosity and love for ancient places and objects, devouring information about and images of ancient civilizations. The result is art that is archeological in nature, mysterious in design, and reverent in interpretation. Each project is an adventure as I continue in my pursuit of information and experiences. Along with fiber, I've also developed an interest in photography. I frequently roam the museums and galleries of New York City. In these and other excursions, I photograph old buildings, ruins and objects that capture my imagination. By combining the historical information I've gathered, I then begin my journey searching for repetition of patterns from the distant past and recent past. In the words of Carl Jung, "What is stirred in us is that faraway background, those immemorial patterns of the human mind, which we have not acquired but have inherited from the dim ages of the past."

I've been sewing since I was 12, but started quilting about seven years ago after experimenting in various media. I moved from traditional to art quilts with the discovery that I loved the texture that is inherent in textile art. I knew then I had found my niche. Initially using bright colors, I've mellowed and now prefer muted colors which give the illusion of a patina of age.

I'm proud to be part of Quilt 21, especially since the opening is in Lowell, MA and I grew up nearby. Lowell shows all that can be done with the ruins of the past, and is now a spectacular city ready for the future, but keeping all the important characteristics of yesterday. My home town of Lawrence has not been revitalized as Lowell has, hopefully some day it will shine again.

Thanks to Director Maxine Farkas for all the long hard hours she's put into making Q21 a reality, and because of her efforts making it the prestigious exhibit it has quickly become. Also a heartfelt thank you to this year's Jurors, Laura Cater-Woods and Maxine Farkas for thinking that my humble work deserved this honor.

The Quilts

Joanie Gagnon San Chirico
Altar Fragments VI: Eclipse
Jurors' Choice Award

I'm intrigued by the combination of old and new, the ancient and the unknown and love working with the texture that is inherent in fabric. My art is archeological in nature and since people of the past intertwined their culture and religions, some may perceive that I make spiritual art. It's obvious to me why ancient people considered the moon and sun as religious entities, and the unexplainable was made to be supernatural.

I've simplified the design from other pieces in my Artifacts series, down to the basic level, from arches, columns and altars, into fragments. The background fabric, dyed by Helene Davis, insisted on manifesting itself as an Eclipse.

Altar Fragments VI: Eclips
20" x 30

Michele Merges Martens
Seaweed Nightmare

Seaweed growing in the ocean is very organic . . . curves and wavy lines, circles and bubbles, even washed up on shore the patterns are rounded. The strands have a curious kind of freedom to choose how they form the patterns. The nightmare is when they dream of being forced into rigid lines and boxes.

Seaweed Nightmare
28" x 39"

Judith Trager
Bosque Sunrise

My work is a continual effort to stretch the limits of landscape and narrative. These concepts are often parallel, and as often, they merge, coalesce, and synthesize. I seek to celebrate the complexity and ambiguity of the metaphorical contemporary Western landscape. To achieve this, I am willing to use any technique which suits my purpose: patchwork, painting, layering, applique, beading, embroidery—literally anything which gives texture, form, and substance to my quilts. My willingness to experiment sometimes makes my work uneven, but never dull. My landscapes are those of dreams and immediacy, my narratives are of past lives and future commitments. Reality has never hampered my work.

Bosque Sunrise
28" x 40"

Catherine Kleeman
Indian Summer

Not a day goes by that I am not bombarded by inspiration from my greatest design resource—the natural world. It is a continuous starting place of new images and color combinations and interesting shapes. The changing of the seasons makes me eager to see what new surprises are displayed outside my door. Traveling through the countryside and watching the landscape unfold makes my heart sing and makes me eager to get back to my fabric palette. Natural and man-made structures tempt me with both repetition and diversity. Yet when one views my work, it is not immediately evident that these are my inspirations; my work is an abstraction of the concepts and a simplification of the design.

"Indian Summer" was created in the autumn when I was surrounded by trees turning shades of fiery red, burnt orange, and brilliant yellow, all against a background of muted greens and russets. I had been playing with vertical and horizontal structural elements in previous works, and continued that design in this piece. I enjoyed the effect of the irregular shape of the piece. And I hope that I have conveyed the colors of autumn within the haziness of an Indian Summer.

>
Indian Summer
30" x 25"

Rosemary Hoffenberg
First Quarter

Nonverbal communication produces an impact which touches each
viewer differently. The shapes are reminiscent of other things.
Working improvisationally, I seek to incorporate lines and color
into a cohesive design.

First Quarter
22" x 31"

Joan Lockburner Deuel
Downtown

Light and shadows, angles and curves, odd color juxtapositions and
word/idea contrasts are my personal challenges in creating an art quilt.
I orchestrate color, line and form in my work by dyeing, painting or
printing the fabric, manipulating the surface with collage or piecing, and
creating texture and depth through my choice of quilting design. Although
I am equally comfortable with representational or abstract work, I prefer
the abstract as it offers endless options for interpretive growth.

Downtown
26" x 39"

Helene Davis
Black Rain

Sometimes you all see a butterfly.   Sometimes you can't agree at all.
Sometimes you dip your toes in the water.   Sometimes you reach deep into the well.
Sometimes you follow the bread crumbs.   Sometimes you arrive at alien ground.
Sometimes you meet a piece of your past.   Sometimes your vision precedes reality.
Sometimes you must buy a ticket.   Sometimes you ride for free.
Sometimes it rains when you need it . . . and a quilt germinates.

Black Rain
34" x 35

Carol Taylor
Windows.com

In the high tech world of 2002, you cannot mention the word
"windows" without also thinking of the computer operating system.
Everything is a ".com" these days. So, this quilt's title is really a play
on the word. The wall of pieced "windows" was created by using
hand dyed and discharged fabrics, and embellished by free motion
quilting throughout.

Windows.com
38" x 20

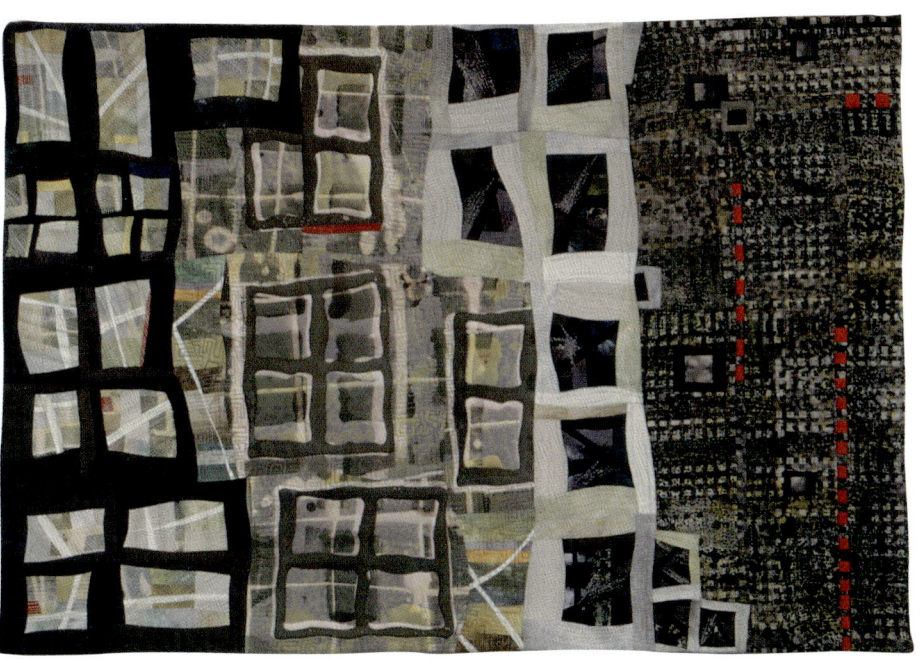

Barbara Pucci
Help/fear #4 (Trapped)

This piece is one in a series of work about empathy that explores isolation and seclusion as well as fear and pain. Using a flowing handwriting script, a lacey pattern is formed with the English words "fear," "suffering," "pain," "wholeness," "veil," and "intimacy" to create an environment of attempted communication and the struggle to express oneself. The style of writing itself is a script used in Germany up until the 1940's.

This series was transformed after the Sept 11th attacks. The focus became the helplessness and fear we all felt around the New York City area, including the Jewish and Arabic communities. Using an online translation program, I found words for "help" and "fear" in Hebrew and Arabic. These were then printed graphically over the handwriting in long trains, reminiscent of a tallis, or prayer shawl, to speak for all of us caught in the crossfire of the world's anger and rage.

Help/Fear #4 (Trapped)
21" x 34

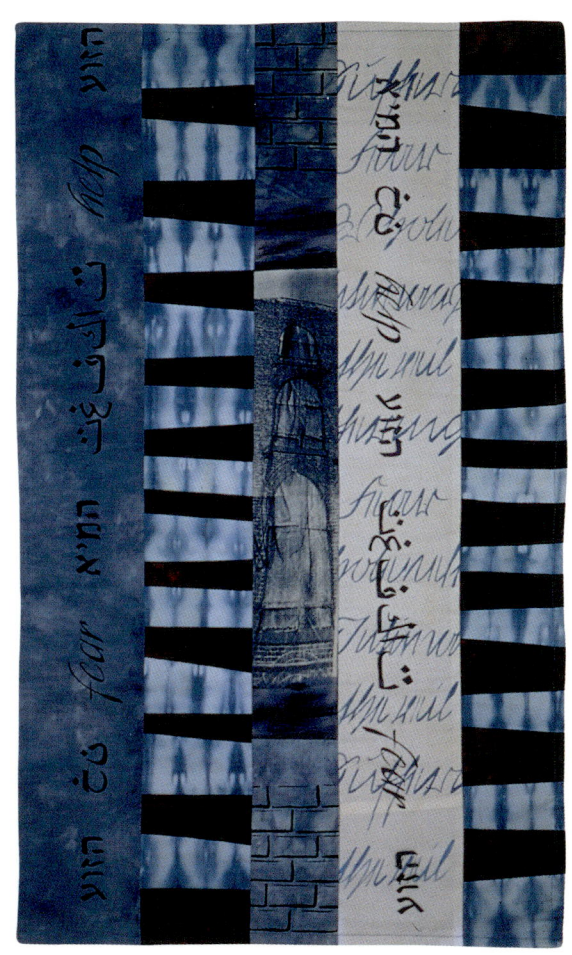

Joan Schulze
The Cloisters

The Cloisters is a 'composted' collage quilt. It is composed by taking
an earlier work, cutting it up and recycling it to make a new quilt.
This takes the idea of collage and extends it to a risky enterprise. I
could be left with beautiful pieces that do not coalesce. The final act
of composting was to draw on the quilt with machine stitches. As
I moved over the surface of the quilt, I had the feeling of actually
working in the cloister's garden. What is compost and what is
original? You decide.

The Cloister
36" x 40

Rayna Gillman
Urban Landscape

Fascinated by printmaking and frustrated with earlier efforts on paper,
I began in 2000 to print on fabric. Using monoprinting (with a press
and by hand), screenprinting, dyeing, painting, photo transfer, and a
variety of materials I worked until my collection reached a critical
mass. Then, this quilt seemed to make itself.

Urban Landscape is the first major work to incorporate both my quilt
and printmaking skills and with this piece, I have found my "voice."

⊳
Urban Landscape
40" x 34"

Pat Autenrieth
Myopia

Using varied printmaking applications, I always print an image on
different fabrics for future use. They are combined with other
similarly stockpiled images in many ways until new meanings emerge.
Then new elements—commercially printed fabrics (I abhor chemistry),
stitching, and more printmaking—are added to resolve a work.
Myopia is typical of this working method.

Myopi
30" x 24

Linda Colsh
Embers

In the aftermath of the Pebble Beach fire, pine cones that burst in the heat cast out the seeds of a new forest. I saw in this a metaphor for the creative process: each work contains the seeds of future creations; some of the seeds will come to nothing, but a few will grow into new works or the next direction, style or exploration.

This quilt is the first in a series on the creative process. The female figure is a statue I photographed and a silkscreen was then made from the photograph. She is an artistic muse. Interestingly, when I researched the Classical muses, there is no muse for the visual arts; they were the muses of music, literature and drama.

Ember
27" x 21"

Denise Linet
Abstraction #4

My husband spilt the orange juice this morning,
As the rays of sunshine lit the distant hills golden.

A chickadee beat its wings against my window,
        Looking for seeds
The feeder swung empty in the breeze.

As I had visions of planes
        Falling from the sky,
      Flames leaping ———— smoke billowing
     Like hope, ashes blowing in the wind.

By afternoon the juice dried sticky on my floor,
A reminder of the promise each morning brings.

Abstraction #4
21" x 25

Eliza Brewster
Window From Tomorrow

I have been fascinated for a long time by the juxtaposition of
indoors\outdoors in the world we live in. I have been working on this
concept for quite some years. My method of conceiving and then
working out is totally by instinct . . . I never know how things will
say what I want them to say but in this quilt I am coming close !!!

Window From Tomorrow
34" x 36"

Victoria Montgomery
Cloth Sketches I: Passé

 . . . a reflection on my work, a distillation of what I do, celebratory and personal, forging an introspective bridge between myself and the observer . . .

my inspirational muse: discovering the extraordinary in the commonplace, shaped from the interior outward as mood sets direction and emphasis responding to the visual, images touching the imagination evoking a sharp statement reaching out to the spirit and emotions of the observer, remaining honest to detail, yet open to new techniques addressing the self, above all.

this piece—Cloth Sketches I: Passé: neglected society, thought passé, outdated, obsolete, touches me, speaks to me strongly of silent agony, a departure in technique, simple graphite renderings, aesthetic sketches imaging the bold through subtle gradations between panels, that visage, that image, that gaze a lifeís narration in reflection ageless beauty, ésprit forte, wisdom illusive and enigmatic contemplative, adoring, pensive, whose, the scrutiny, where the thought ?

Cloth Sketches I: Pas
30" x 19

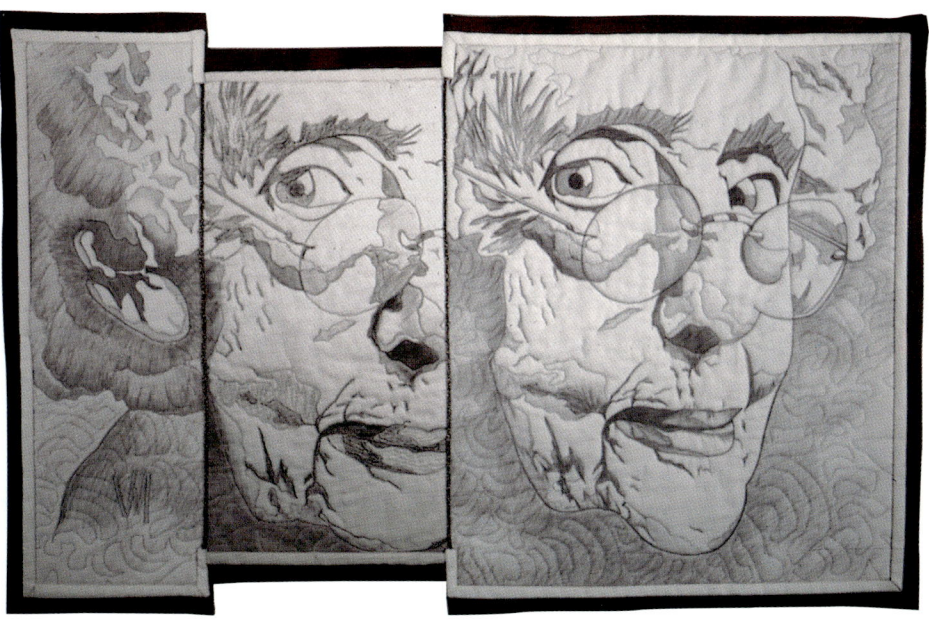

Susan Shie and James Acord
The Car Handover

We bought a new car on July 24, 2001. This piece is about letting go of our beloved old car and bonding with our new one. We'd had the old one for a long time, and this was our first brand new car in the whole of our 25 years together at that time.

I began the piece as an airbrush demonstration during our August 2001 Turtle Art Camps. I just put black paint in the airbrush and let 'er rip! I love to work spontaneously! I sandwiched and began to quilt it as more class instruction. And Jimmy used the piece for his machine embroidery demo on my cursive writing. Then I went for a week later in August to Hilton Head Island, with a pack of old and new friends who were all turning 50 within a year of each other, known as Pat's YaYas. When I got back, I was still sewing away, of course, but decided to stop at some point, because I'm trying to paint more and stitch less.

>
The Car Handover
38" x 23"

We bought Babycakes in late June, 95, from our friends Kenny + Mary Helen. She's a 1990 Isuzu Trooper. the little gray pakiderm Babycakes

We just now bought Aunt Louise July 24, 2001. She's a new 2001 Subaru Outback. from Waikem in Massillon.

good car safe ★ 205,000 miles on her

blessings

Eric Mayle was our nice Libra salesman. Mama Wanda drove & forgot the mileage!!!

TURTLE PIE HONEY BUTTER

alias Madamoiselle Kissey

TROOPER

Aunt Louise

OUTBACK CD player + thing 1

Hattie was born around the same day we bought Babycakes. July 26, 96. Painting started July 27, 2001

HATTIE

Marigold will love riding in the new car, if she has to go to the vet.

Marigold I'm not sick

©Susan Shie 2001

©Susan Shie 2001

Painting begun July 24, 01

53

Kathy Nida
Caught in the Headlights

Once upon a time, a long time ago, in a land far, far away, there lived a princess and her trusty Palm Pilot. There's something about being female, and being a Mom, and being a wife, and working out of the house, and trying to go back to school, and trying to be an artist. There's something about being caught in the headlights.

First I draw with pen on paper (no erasing allowed), then I trace to fusible web, cut, iron, sew like the dickens, attach whatever bits and pieces are within reach, and then, then I go on to the next one.

>
Caught in the Headlights
30" x 38"

Marni Goldshlag
How Many Words is a Picture Worth?

I am intrigued by the use of words in visual art. I wonder whether the words need to contain meaning or function simply as interesting marks. "How Many Words is a Picture Worth?" contains meaningful words in several languages as well as marks that imply language, but aren't. Do I need to learn Arabic and Japanese in order to use these languages in a meaningful way in my art or can I simply use meaningless marks that are similar to these languages? And if they are meaningless, does the work require a picture to give it meaning?

How Many Words is a Picture Worth
20" x 28

Joan Loewenberg
No Longer Safe

I am a cold war child. I remember junior high school nuclear air raid
drills. When the Berlin Wall fell, I thought our global world would
become a safer and freer place for all. I made a quilt with my own
hand printed birds and my husband's old shirts to symbolize an
optimistic future. Over the ensuing years, my optimism faded as did
my quilt. September 11th occurred, and it is clear that none of us are
free or safe from the hatred of "other." As I mourned for those lost
and feared that current solutions will birth only more pain and hatred
into this world, I dismantled the old faded quilt and put it together
with new materials. Birds that once flew free are shown trapped or
caught in netting, used to symbolize fear, prejudice and oppression.
I am left with the question: How do we create a world that truly
honors the inherent worth and dignity of all peoples?

No Longer Safe
35" x 34"

Julie John Upshaw
Worms and Holes I
Husqvarna Viking Award for 2002

The question I am most often asked is some form of, "What's with the worms?" Until a year ago I did not even call the tubular forms in my work "worms." Over the years the worm forms have been bugs, blobs, legs, human forms, larvae, vacuum hoses, water wiggles, an umbilical cord, brain matter, and germs. This is the first series where I call these forms "worms."

Worms and Holes I marks a change in my work. The majority of my work is humorous or absurd. When I started this new series I had a strong desire for my work to be viewed a little more seriously, and that just does not happen when people are laughing out loud. Sometimes in life we get a new haircut and outfit to mark an inward difference we are feeling. That same urge was central to this piece.

With my worms dressed up, I felt free to run with the rest. Sewing large holes in layers of fabric, machine drawing with black thread, and machine embroidery on organza, are all elements of my current work. In Worms and Holes I the final result is a seven-layer quilt that you can see all the way through. It is meant to be viewed in the round.

Worms and Holes
15" x 1"

Randy Keenan
The Armchair Traveler

My Grandmother had heart trouble so she did not get around much.
She got the word out and every week when she attended mass her
friends slipped her glassine envelopes full of exotic stamps from all
over the world: Tanzania, Ceylon, Gibraltar, Guyana, Toga, etc.
Can you imagine just how vast the world was in those days without
all of our technology? But this retired English teacher traveled the
world from her armchair!

Fifty years later I found her stamp collection in Papa's old wooden
cigar box overflowing with all these little graphic jewels. The years
warped and I connected with her immediately. As a very little girl
I thought her a rather severe and imposing woman, but she sent me
this gift over time and space and it allowed me to travel the world
from my armchair! Thanks Grandma.

The Armchair Travel
20" x 2

Linda Levin
Bilbao I

Bilbao I is a part of a series inspired by a trip to see the Guggenheim
Museum in Bilbao, Spain, designed by Frank Gehry. It's composed
of interrelated curving forms sheathed in brushed titanium which
reflects light in extraordinary ways and changes depending on weather
and time of day.

I used layers of different sheer, lustrous fabrics over shiny satin to
capture the wonderfully changeable surface. My goal was to find the
spirit of the building rather than to try to render it literally. The eye
wants to wander among the concave and convex forms and follow the
ever-changing patterns of light and shadow.

Bilbao
29" x 40

Phil D. Jones
Night Falling

I love transforming raw materials into objects of beauty and contemplation. At some point, the materials come together to form something greater than the sum of the parts. It's then when I ask: "Is this what I imagined? Does it embody the spirit and energy I envisioned? Did I get out of the way and allow this work to bloom?" This is the process for me. Inevitably, the work speaks about the relationship of my inner thoughts and feelings to the outer world.

"Night Falling" is the third in a series of work that explores using handmade silk paper and other fibers in an applique-like process. I love the luminosity and texture provided by these materials. This piece represents that rare moment-within-a-moment that captures the essence of nightfall, that instant when the day bows its head to the glorious coming of evenings magic.

Night Fallin
22" x 4C

Dan Olfe
Caribbean Sunset

The quilt Caribbean Sunset is the smallest quilt in a current series containing horizontal or vertical stripes with widths varying from 1/8" to 1". These works are inspired by nature, music, and modern artists who have painted stripes (like Gene Davis, Kenneth Nolan, and Bridget Riley).

My early quilts were cotton wall hangings that were machine pieced and quilted. My later works are whole cloth quilts made of cotton poplin. They are hand-painted with transparent textile paints, and then machine quilted. Painting allows me to control the colors and incorporate small details. My abstract geometric designs are inspired by native art, modern and contemporary paintings, special tiling patterns, architecture, science, and technology. I fine tune the designs on a computer to achieve desired shapes and colors.

Caribbean Sunse
39" x 39

Judy Becker
Thanks to Elizabeth

Some house guests bring flowers, chocolates, or a bottle of wine.
Elizabeth Barton, a talented artist and perceptive friend, brought her
silk-screened fabric. We were staying at the beach in Rhode Island
and the dark mysterious material reminded me of vegetation under the
sea. Thanks again, Elizabeth.

Thanks to Elizabeth
38" x 33'

Linda Colsh
Fall Line

Starting with three of my photographs, one of the Hoge Bos (High
Forest) near my home in Belgium and two of laundry I shot in China,
I cropped and "stitched" the three images together via computer. I
further altered the composite image on the computer, printed it out
and transferred it to fabric.

My idea to put laundry in a forest is based on "Rauschenbergish"
principles of combining objects and places that are not really together
in an "assemblage," creating the absurd, the dreamlike. Images like
the one I created for this quilt sometimes flash onto the screen that
exists in my mind. They are very private places because they exist
only in my imagination.

Laundry (a theme I have used before) is "women's banner." Men
parade in the streets with flags and bunting; women's equivalent is a
line heavy with clean laundry, flapping and fresh in the wind.

Fall Lin
23" x 23

Wen Redmond
Behind The Shadow, Waiting To Shine

Working with fabric, color and texture has always been a source of jubilation for me. I manipulate and embellish material to create innovative assemblages on quilts and one of a kind wearables. I seek to tap into levels of myself and when I teach, to help others do the same—to reach deep inside and bring up . . . ourselves. I allow the fabrics I work with to focus me intuitively. Each piece seems to have an expression of it's own. I act as the facilitator. The works begin as an idea from nature or a dream, a treasured moment or insight. Thus inspired and wrought with joy, they become real. A sweet fruition of spirit.

Behind the Shadow, Waiting to Shine
20" x 25"

Sandra L. H. Woock
Cosmic Matters

Cosmic Matters was definitely great fun to create. I relied on a childish/playful concept of space without the major research and study required to make it a factual statement. I want to illustrate a notion of mystery, power and color. What colors do we see in space? In this case it doesn't matter; I had fun making the choice.

Cosmic Matte
40" x 4(

Claire Fenton
Fences 9
Pfaff Artists Award for Excellence

I am intrigued by fences in all their variations: intricate wrought iron,
neat white pickets, rustic and decaying wood, beach fences . . . even
rows of trees. They represent boundary, order, timelessness; they
reflect the history and soul of place

Fences
30" x 3(

Sandra Townsend Donabed
Coleus Mandela

I have always sewn and I have also always been an artist, but it wasn't
until I was long into adult life that I had one of those moments of
synchronicity that made me realize I could combine both as my
medium of choice.

For my work, the fabric is generally the focus. I usually start with a
piece that speaks to me and take off from there—the stories develop
in my subconscious as I work, much like Tanguay's 'automatic
writing'. In fact, when I finish a piece I rarely remember the process
of making it but I do know the associations and the stories that give it
meaning. I really don't feel like I make these pieces, they simply
come through me using my technique and craft to become whole.

My newer work has focused on exploring printmaking techniques,
both hand pulled and computer generated, depending upon the need of
the image. 'Coleus Mandela' was constructed of fabric printed on my
ink jet printer from digital photographs manipulated from my original
files. All my work has a back-story, I never just focus on line or color
for it's own sake, this piece is about my overgrown garden of colorful
foliage in Florida. I have gotten further and further from traditional
quilt-making, but I just cannot give up working with layers and
stitchery. I hope I never do.

Coleus Mandela
30" x 30

Sara Rockinger
Dandelions
Bernina Award for Innovation in Machine Embroidery

I think of quilts as painters think of canvases. I push the limits of my
canvas by taking it off the stretcher, layering, stitching, unraveling,
deconstructing, and integrating color by dyeing, stamping, and
painting. I am process oriented and let the evolving piece speak to me
as I go. I choose subject matter like dandelions because they are
marginalized, tenacious, and quite often the only things blooming in
my garden. How grateful I am for any splash of color.

Making art in the form of quilts is a double-edged sword. It is at once
a more accessible form of art, yet instantly reduced in stature when
you take it off the frame. I have studied painting, drawing,
photography, pottery and fiber arts, and have been a quilter and fiber
artist for more than 12 years. The cutting edge art quilt and textile
movement inspires me, and women's rich textile history roots me in
the passion, creativity and adversity of my foremothers.

I was originally inspired by the realists of Rembrandt's era. Later,
Impressionist masters captured my attention and continue to amaze me
and inform my work. Picasso and Matisse thrill me with their
boldness, and Abstractionists move me to anger and awe. But it is
artists such as Margaret Burke White, Judy Chicago, Mary Cassatt and
Cindy Sherman who fuel my passion for art making. For me, they
capture, honor, and address head on their experiences of life as
women. Their art has given me permission to pursue my own vision
and purpose.

Dandelion
15" x 1

Cornelia Jutta Forster
Autumn Meditation

Late autumn is a time when life centers itself. Energy is drawn to the core where it gathers, circulates and sustains. Nonessentials are eliminated and skeletal strength remains. From this internal focus there are echoed reflections to the periphery.

Autumn Meditation
25" x 30

Dominie Nash
Particolare 6 and 7

The Particolare Series

I find that looking closely at a small section of an artwork can increase
my appreciation of that work. In addition, it offers the bonus of
revealing another composition within the larger work, having a life of
its own. This series takes as a starting point such detailed views of my
own recent work, which are then blown up; the colors often change
and the shapes may be broken up into smaller segments, but the overall
structure remains the same. There is always a moment of surprise (and
truth) when a 12" section becomes an entity many times that size.

Particolare (
40" x 40

Particolare 7
40" x 40"

Materials Appendix
Information on materials supplied by artists.

Eliza Brewster
Window From Tomorrow
Cotton, photo-transfer, perm markers, color discharge, hand sewn, hand applique.

Linda Colsh
Embers
Cotton fabrics, resisted, discharged, screen-printed, stamped and injection over dyed by the artist. Machine pieced, machine quilted.

Linda Colsh
Fall Line
Cotton, silk and "eyelash" fabrics, many dyed, painted, discharged and silkscreened by the artist. Photo transfer of images manipulated and combined on the computer. Machine pieced, machine quilted.

Joan Deuel
Downtown
Artist dyed cotton broadcloth, machine pieced, machine quilted, embroidery.

Claire Fenton
Fences 9
fused, machine stitched, hand-dyed and painted, commercial fabrics, decorative threads

Cornelia Jutta Forster
Autumn Meditation
Silk upholstery fabric, cottons, sheers; fusible web, acrylic paint; rayon, nylon and cotton threads; embroidery floss and specialty yarn; beads and found objects.

Marni Goldshlag
How Many Words is a Picture Worth
Untreated canvas painted with color concentrates (and a few pieces of airbrush painted canvas), pieced with Lunn Studios "naughty ladies" screenprints (colored with markers), sheer overlays.

Rosemary Hoffenberg
First Quarter
Hand dyed and commercial cottons, canvas, block and screen printed, machine pieced, machine quilted.

Phil D. Jones
Night Falling
Hand-dyed and painted cotton fabric, cotton batting, handmade silk paper, silk, wool and other fibers, rayon and metallic thread, monofilament, direct applique, machine quilted.

Randy Keenan
The Armchair Traveler
Hand dyed fabric, vellum stencils,
navy netting with lapis sparkle
chips, scanned images of stamps
and clock faces printed on hand
dyed fabric and machine quilted
onto the surface.

Catherine Kleeman
Indian Summer
Cotton fabric, both commercial and
hand dyed by the artist; raw edge
machine appliqué, machine and
hand quilting.

Linda Levin
Bilbao I
Composed of several layers of
transparent fabrics to give the
effect of changing light on the
titanium surface of the building.
The stitching follows the contours
of the curving forms.

Denise Linet
Abstraction #4
Machine pieced, raw edge
applique, fused using hand dyed
fabrics, & xerography, machine
quilted.

Michele Merges Martens
Seaweed Nightmare
Fabric and fibers hand-dyed by the
artist, buttons, beads, sequins,
found objects, holographic foil.
Machine quilted.

Dominie Nash
Particolare 6 and 7
Cotton and silk, machine applique
and quilting, multiple surface
design processes by the artist.

Kathy Nida
Caught in the Headlights
Fused, machine appliqued and
quilted, hand embroidered and
beaded, hand-dyed and commercial
fabrics.

Dan Olfe
Caribbean Sunset
Whole cloth quilt of cotton poplin;
painted by hand with transparent
textile paints, machine quilted.

Barbara Pucci
Help/fear #4 (Trapped)
Hand dyed cotton fabric, acrylic
paint, and oil-based printing inks.
Cyanotype photograph, and
pochoir.

Wen Redmond
Behind the Shadow, Waiting to Shine
Dyed cottons, machine quilting and
embroidery, curved piecing and
free applique.

Sara Rockinger
Dandelions
Whole cloth quilt, hand dyed
cotton fabric and gauze, machine
appliqued and embroidered.

Joan Schulze
The Cloisters
silk, cotton, paper, lace transfer and
photographic processes, appliqué,
machine stitching

Susan Shie and James Acord
The Car Handover
Two panels: each
23"h x 19"w. Whole cloth
paintings, mostly hand
embroidered over the airbrush
work, and using my Lucky School
of Quilting Techniques.
Embellishments include mostly
buttons and bugle beads.

Carol Taylor
Windows.com
hand dyed and discharged fabrics,
and embellished by free motion
quilting throughout.

Judith Trager
Bosque Sunrise
Cotton and silk. Machine pieced
and appliqued. Machine quilted.

Sandra L. H. Woock
Cosmic Matters
Cotton, resist/discharged,
dyepainted, whole cloth
construction, machine quilted

INDEX

Images denoted in bold.